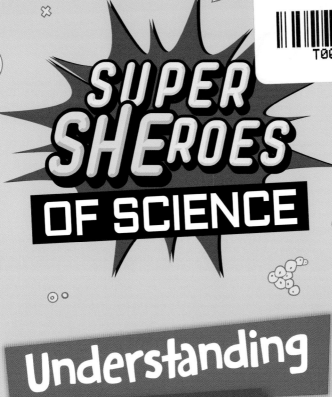

Super SHEROES OF SCIENCE

Understanding Earth

Women Who Led the Way

NANCY DICKMANN

Children's Press®
An imprint of Scholastic Inc.

Library of Congress Cataloging-in-Publication Data

Names: Dickmann, Nancy, author.

Title: Understanding Earth : women who led the way / Nancy Dickmann.

Description: First edition. | New York : Children's Press, an imprint of
  Scholastic Inc., 2022. | Series: Super SHEroes of science | Includes bibliographical references and index. |
  Audience: Ages 8-10. | Audience: Grades 4-6. | Summary: "This brand-new series highlights some of the major
  contributions women have made in the world of science. Photographs throughout"— Provided by publisher.

Identifiers: LCCN 2021037051 (print) | LCCN 2021037052 (ebook) | ISBN 9781338800500 (library binding) |
  ISBN 9781338800517 (paperback) | ISBN 9781338800524 (ebk)

Subjects: LCSH: Women earth scientists—Biography—Juvenile literature. | Women scientists—
  Biography—Juvenile literature. | Earth sciences—Biography—Juvenile literature. |
  BISAC: JUVENILE NONFICTION / Biography & Autobiography / Women Classification: LCC QE21 .D53 2022 (print) |
  LCC QE21 (ebook) | DDC 509.2/52—dc23

LC record available at https://lccn.loc.gov/2021037051

LC ebook record available at https://lccn.loc.gov/2021037052

Picture credits:

Photos ©: cover top: Science Source; cover center top: Images & Volcans/Science Source; cover center bottom: Jeff Miller/University of Wisconsin-Madison; cover bottom: Courtesy of Dail St. Claire; 5 left: Science Source; 5 center left: Images & Volcans/Science Source; 5 center right: Jeff Miller/University of Wisconsin-Madison; 5 right: Courtesy of Dail St. Claire; 6 inset top: Pictorial Press Ltd/Alamy Images; 7 top: Richard T. Nowitz/Getty Images; 8 top: Carlyn Iverson/NOAA Climate.gov; 10 bottom: Artur Widak/NurPhoto/Getty Images; 11 top: American Journal of Science/NOAA Climate.gov; 12 inset top: Science Source; 13 bottom: Impress/Alamy Images; 14 top right: World History Archive/Alamy Images; 15 top: Photo Josse/Bridgeman Images; 16 top: Look and Learn/Bridgeman Images; 16 bottom: Photos.com/Getty Images; 17 top: Culture Club/Getty Images; 18 top left: The Print Collector/Alamy Images; 20 inset top: Hoa-Qui/Krafft/Science Source; 21 right: Giovanni Isolino/AFP/Getty Images; 22 bottom: Bella Falk/Alamy Images; 23 top: Explorer/Krafft/Science Source; 24 top: Reuters/Alamy Images; 24 bottom: Jackyenjoyphotography/Getty Images; 25 top: by Mike Lyvers/Getty Images; 26 top left: Images & Volcans/Science Source; 26 bottom left: Dorling Kindersley ltd/Alamy Images; 28 inset top: Wendy Mao; 31 top: Linda A. Cicero/Stanford News Service; 34 top: Courtesy of Dail St. Claire; 35 top: Geological Sciences/Flickr; 36 top: FineArt/Alamy Images; 36 bottom: SPL/Science Source; 37 top: Science Source; 38 top: Bettmann/Getty Images; 39 top: The Granger Collection; 39 bottom: Vassar College/Flickr; 40 top left: National Library of Medicine/Science Source; 40 bottom left: FineArt/Alamy Images; 41 top right: wataru aoki/Getty Images; 42-43: pop_jop/Getty Images; 44 top left: Science Source; 44 bottom left: Images & Volcans/Science Source; 45 top: Wendy Mao.

All other photos © Shutterstock.

10 9 8 7 6 5 4 3 2 1   22 23 24 25 26

Printed in the U.S.A. 113
First edition, 2022
Series produced for Scholastic by Parcel Yard Press

Contents

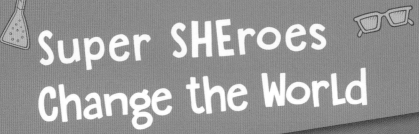

Super SHEroes Change the World

Women scientists, engineers, and inventors have made remarkable breakthroughs for centuries. Often, however, their achievements went unrecognized. Today far more women work in these fields than ever before, and their achievements are celebrated.

This book celebrates the life and the work of twelve of these women, twelve Super SHEroes of Science! They all worked, or still work, trying to understand Earth.

Earth is the planet where we live. In order to understand Earth, scientists study its structure, composition, and climate. They also study its history, trying to discover everything that has happened since it was formed 4.5 billion years ago.

SUPER SHEROES OF SCIENCE

Marie Curie

Katia Krafft

Sau Lan Wu

June Bacon-Bercey

The Super SHEroes of Science in this book have figured out what is going on deep inside our planet, studied erupting volcanoes, and made incredible discoveries about **atoms**, the tiny units that everything on Earth is made of. And many of these women started off by being told that science wasn't for them. But they stuck to their dreams, asked questions, and took risks. They eventually got to write their own stories.

This book brings their stories to you! And while you read them, remember:

Your story can change the world, too! You can become a Super SHEro of Science.

Eunice Newton Foote

Eunice Newton Foote studied the way that different kinds of gases in the air trap the sun's heat. Today, her pioneering work helps us understand **climate change**.

Eunice was born into a large family and grew up in Upstate New York. Her father was a farmer. At the age of about seventeen, Eunice went to a school 200 miles from her home. She lived and studied at the school and only went home for the holidays.

datafile

Born: 1819

Died: 1888

Place of birth: United States

Role: Physicist

Super SHEro for: Discovering the natural process behind the greenhouse effect

Eunice's school taught science, which was very unusual for a girls' school at the time. Eunice learned how to carry out scientific experiments.

When Eunice got married, she and her husband moved to Seneca Falls, New York, where they raised two daughters. In 1848, a meeting was held in the town, called the Women's Rights Convention. People from all over America came to discuss the rights of women and whether women should be able to do the same jobs men did. The convention published a list of ideas about changing the lives of all women. The public was asked to sign the list to show they agreed. Eunice was one of the first in line.

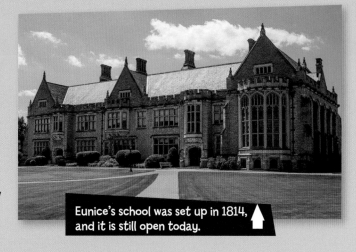

Eunice's school was set up in 1814, and it is still open today.

What's Your Story?

One of the teachers at Eunice's school was Almira Hart Lincoln Phelps. She wrote science books that were popular with the students. Eunice may have read them and been inspired by them to be a scientist!

Which books have inspired you?

Why did you like them?

Eunice set up an experiment to investigate how the gases in the air became warmer.

Eunice and her husband, Elisha, worked on science experiments together in their spare time. In the 1850s, **geologists** were discovering many new fossils. They suggested that millions of years ago, Earth's climate was much warmer. But what had caused the warm temperatures? And why was Earth cooler now? Eunice decided to do simple experiments to find out more.

Fossils give us clues about what the world was like a long time ago.

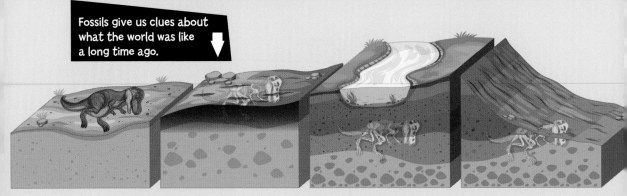

She put thermometers into glass jars and filled the jars with different kinds of gases found in the air. She then put them in the sunshine and recorded the temperature every few minutes as the gases warmed up. She discovered that **carbon dioxide** (CO_2) and water vapor (also called steam) heated up fastest. She realized that adding these gases to the **atmosphere** could make the planet warmer—and taking them away made it colder.

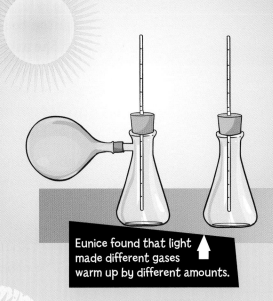

Eunice found that light made different gases warm up by different amounts.

Did You Know?

Light from the sun shines through the atmosphere and warms up Earth. However, some of the gases in the air, especially carbon dioxide, stop some of Earth's heat from going back out into space. This is called the greenhouse effect, and it keeps the planet warm. By burning fuels, like gasoline, people are adding extra carbon dioxide to the air. This is making Earth warm up and is causing climate change.

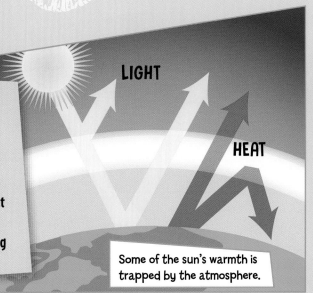

LIGHT

HEAT

Some of the sun's warmth is trapped by the atmosphere.

Eunice wanted to share her results with other scientists. She asked to talk about her discovery at an important science conference in 1856. But as a woman, she was not allowed to. Instead, a male scientist, Joseph Henry, read out a description of her work on Eunice's behalf.

A story about Eunice's work then appeared in *Scientific American* magazine. Even so, most scientists ignored what Eunice had found out. Three years later, the Irish scientist John Tyndall published his own report about carbon dioxide and the way it traps heat. He claimed that this was a new discovery.

Climate change is now a very important issue for the whole world.

Tyndall was already a famous scientist and so his research made the news. For many decades he was seen as one of the founders of climate science. Meanwhile, Eunice continued with new experiments. She published other reports on gas and electricity and also made several inventions.

It was not until 2011 that Eunice's work on gases and the climate was rediscovered. We now know that Eunice was the first person to show the link between gases in the air and Earth's global temperature. **Today, her research has led to activists around the world working to prevent climate change.**

Few scientists read Eunice's scientific paper.

What Would You Do?

As you've just read, another scientist got the credit for Eunice's big discovery. Nevertheless, she did not give up and kept on researching.

Have you ever seen someone else get credit for your work?

What would you do if that happened?

Marie Curie

Marie Curie worked for many years to understand **radioactivity**, an unusual natural process where substances give out invisible rays.

datafile

Born: 1867

Died: 1934

Place of birth: Poland

Field: Physics

Super SHEro for: Discovering two new elements and pioneering the use of radioactivity in medicine

Marie was born in Poland. Her parents were both teachers who encouraged Marie to read and learn. But because she was a girl, Marie wasn't allowed to go to college. Instead, she and her sister Bronya joined a secret school called the "Floating University." Everyone—male and female—was allowed to take classes. Even so, Marie wanted more.

CAFÉ PARIS

In 1891, Marie moved to Paris, France, and joined the famous Sorbonne University there. She studied physics and did very well.

After finishing college Marie wanted to stay in Paris and be a scientist. While she was looking for a laboratory to work in, she met a French scientist named Pierre Curie. They fell in love, got married, and started researching together.

An important discovery had just taken place. A German researcher named Wilhelm Röntgen found invisible rays that could shine through solid objects. He called them X-rays.

The Sorbonne in Paris is still a top university.

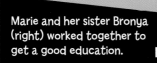

Marie and her sister Bronya (right) worked together to get a good education.

13

The French scientist Henri Becquerel then started searching for more of these mysterious rays. He found them coming out of a rare metal called **uranium**.

Marie was excited by these discoveries. She began looking for other substances that gave off the same invisible rays, also called **radiation**. Marie came up with a name for the mysterious effect: radioactivity.

She studied a rock called pitchblende, which contains some uranium. Marie found that pitchblende was more radioactive than uranium on its own. That meant that at least one of the rock's other parts must be radioactive as well.

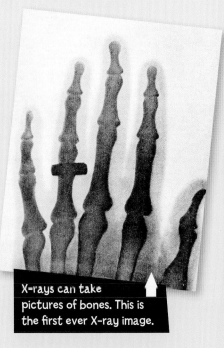

X-rays can take pictures of bones. This is the first ever X-ray image.

What's Your Story?

?

Marie and her sister Bronya made a deal. Marie would work to earn money to pay for Bronya to become a doctor. Then they would swap, and Bronya would pay for Marie's education.

Have you ever made a sacrifice to help a friend?

How did it make you feel?

Marie was determined to find this mystery substance. Pierre joined in to help Marie search. In the end, they were able to find not one, but two new radioactive **elements**.

They called the first one polonium. This name comes from the old Latin word for Poland, Marie's homeland. The second element was called radium, which means "radioactive metal."

Marie and Pierre worked as a team.

Did You Know?

Atoms are the tiny building blocks of all substances. Atoms have a nucleus, or central core. A radioactive atom has a weak nucleus that falls apart easily. When it breaks up, the nucleus gives out rays of energy and particles. This is the process known as radioactivity.

NUCLEUS OF ATOM   RAY

PARTICLE

Marie's discovery made her famous. She was invited to present her work to the Royal Institution in London in 1903. However, only men were allowed to give talks, so Pierre had to do it. Later that year, the couple won the **Nobel Prize** for Physics. They shared the prize with Henri Becquerel, who had also worked with radioactivity.

But just three years later, Pierre was killed in an accident. Marie took over Pierre's place as professor at the Sorbonne. She was the first woman in France to have this job. In 1911 Marie won a second Nobel Prize, this time for her discovery of polonium and radium.

Marie spent long hours using chemicals to purify new elements from minerals.

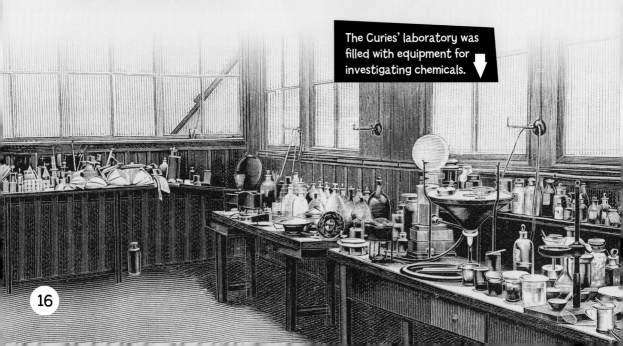

The Curies' laboratory was filled with equipment for investigating chemicals.

It was soon discovered that radioactivity could have many important uses. During World War I, Marie built mobile X-ray machines to help doctors see the injuries inside soldiers' bodies during battles. She trained women to operate them. The machines saved many lives.

After the war, Marie set up a team of researchers, called the Institut Curie, to study how to treat illnesses such as cancer using radioactivity. **This and Marie Curie's other achievements have inspired many women around the world to become a scientist like her.**

Marie's daughter Irène (left) helped with experiments. Irène Joliot-Curie won her own Nobel Prize in 1935.

What Would You Do?

Marie was the first woman to discover new chemical elements and she found ways to use science to help people.

What discovery would you like to make?

How would you use science to make the world a better place?

At Work with Marie Curie

Marie Curie's Paris lab is now a public museum. It is safe to visit. All the dangerous radioactive materials have been cleaned out.

Marie spent long hours working in her laboratory. Compared to modern labs, Marie's workplace was very simple.

Marie and Pierre set up their laboratory in a glass-roofed shed. It was hot and sticky in the summer and cold in the winter, and the rain often got in through leaks. Their chemistry apparatus was set up on simple wooden tables.

There are only tiny amounts of radium and polonium in pitchblende crystals. Separating them was very hard work. Marie stirred big pots of pitchblende, using strong chemicals to wash away the unwanted material. Pierre invented a detector called an electrometer that used electricity to test for radioactivity. It took more than three years to make a few specks of radium weighing 0.004 ounces (0.1 grams).

At night, the radioactivity made the equipment in the lab glow in the dark. Today we know that radioactivity can be very dangerous. But at the time, because it was a new discovery, no one knew. Marie and Pierre did not wear protective equipment when holding radioactive substances like scientists do today. Both of them suffered from health problems because of the radiation traveling through their bodies. In fact, their notebooks are still so radioactive 100 years later that they have to be kept inside strong metal boxes.

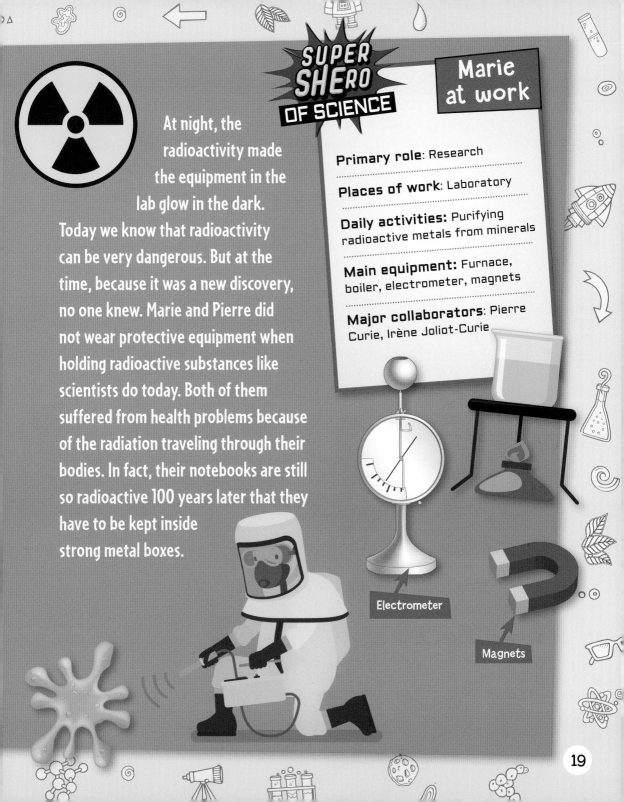

SUPER SHERO OF SCIENCE

Marie at work

Primary role: Research

Places of work: Laboratory

Daily activities: Purifying radioactive metals from minerals

Main equipment: Furnace, boiler, electrometer, magnets

Major collaborators: Pierre Curie, Irène Joliot-Curie

Electrometer

Magnets

Katia Krafft

Katia Krafft was a **vulcanologist**, a scientist who studies volcanoes. She traveled the world examining **craters** and watching eruptions. She wasn't afraid to put herself in danger to learn more about them.

SUPER SHERO OF SCIENCE

Katia was born in France. This is not an area known for its volcanoes. However, when Katia was seventeen, she saw a film about volcanic eruptions. She was fascinated by the subject! She decided to study vulcanology, even though at the time it was seen as a job only for men.

datafile

Born: 1942

Died: 1991

Place of birth: France

Field: Vulcanology

Super SHEro for: Filming and studying volcanic eruptions

Katia studied geology at college. While she was there, she met a fellow student named Maurice Krafft. He was just as fascinated by volcanoes as Katia was. After they graduated, they went to Stromboli, a volcano rising out of the sea near Italy. It was the first time Katia had seen an eruption.

Katia and Maurice collected gases and minerals from near the crater. It was a dangerous job. Volcanic gases are hot, and some are poisonous when breathed in. There is constant danger from falling lava rocks.

The Stromboli volcano has been erupting slowly for several hundred years.

What's Your Story?

Katia and Maurice got married and spent their adult lives traveling the world, studying volcanic eruptions. Their fascination with volcanoes made them a great team.

Have you ever worked as part of a team?

How would you get a team to work together better?

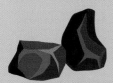

Katia and Maurice gave lectures, wrote books, and shared their films of volcanic eruptions. The money they raised paid for their travels. Whenever a volcano erupted, they went there as soon as possible. Katia's main job was to take photographs of the eruptions. She also took measurements and made scientific observations. By 1987, they had visited more than 300 active volcanoes.

Katia worked inside this crater in Africa, just above a huge lake of burning-hot lava.

Volcano researchers like Katia go right up to the craters of erupting volcanoes to study them. Even if it was a very dangerous job, Katia thought the risks were worth it. She was interested in how and where volcanoes form. She also studied how lava and gases move during an eruption.

Her work kept people safe from eruptions. In 1991, Mount Pinatubo in the Philippines erupted. A video made by the Kraffts was shown to local people and government officials. It convinced everyone to evacuate the area. Many lives were saved.

Katia worked in very dangerous conditions.

Did You Know?

There are pockets of hot, liquid rock called magma deep underground. Volcanoes form when some of this magma breaks through cracks in Earth's surface. As magma reaches the surface, it is called lava. After spreading over the surface, lava cools and hardens into new rock.

The inside of a volcano

Katia and Maurice were willing to do whatever it took to learn more about volcanoes. Once they sailed across a lake in the middle of a volcanic crater—using just a rubber boat! The Kraffts knew how to stay as safe as possible, but volcanoes are always very dangerous.

In 1991, Katia and Maurice traveled to Mount Unzen in Japan, where an eruption had begun. They were two miles from the summit when a flood of hot gas and ash suddenly burst from the crater. Katia and Maurice could not get away before being hit by the deadly cloud. Both were killed instantly by the intense heat.

Katia wore heat-proof metal suits.

The bright blue water in volcanic lakes contains poisonous chemicals.

Mount Unzen gave out a deadly cloud of hot ash.

Thanks to Katia, scientists today know a lot more about the different kinds of lava produced by eruptions. **Vulcanologists can use this information to predict when volcanoes will erupt. This helps keep people safe.**

What Would You Do?

Katia knew that her job was incredibly dangerous but did it anyway so she could make scientific discoveries.

If you were a scientist like Katia, would you be willing to explore an erupting volcano?

Should scientists need to take risks to make new discoveries?

At Work with Katia Krafft

Katia had to get as close as possible to eruptions to gather information about the lava, ash, and gases being released.

Many scientists work in a laboratory. Katia Krafft's lab could be anywhere in the world where a volcano was erupting!

Hard hat

When there was news of an eruption, Katia would pack her equipment and head out with Maurice. Besides the cameras and video cameras to record the eruption, they also took equipment for measuring it. Katia used a tool called a thermocouple to measure the temperature of lava. It has a long metal spike or wires to stick into the lava. The temperature appears on a screen.

Thermocouple

Gas mask

SUPER SHERO OF SCIENCE

Katia at work

One of the most important measurements was finding out which gases were coming out of the volcano. Katia invented a portable version of a tool called a chromatograph. It made it easier to measure gases during eruptions.

Katia needed safety equipment, too. Lava is often hot enough to kill, and even after it has cooled down, lava can be as sharp as glass. Katia wore a body suit made from **asbestos** and metal foil to protect her from the heat. Her boots where heatproof so she could walk across hot ground. A hard hat protected her from flying lumps of rock and lava. She sometimes needed a gas mask to breathe among the poisonous gases.

Primary role: Research

Places of work: Near the craters of erupting volcanoes

Daily activities: Taking measurements and photos of volcanic eruptions

Main equipment: Camera, chromatograph, thermocouples, safety equipment

Main collaborator: Maurice Krafft

Camera

Wendy Mao

SUPER SHERO OF SCIENCE

Thanks to the work of scientists like Wendy Mao, we know a lot about the deep insides of our planet—even though it is impossible to travel there!

Wendy was born in Washington, DC. Her parents had moved from China. Wendy's father was a geologist who came to the United States to study. Wendy and her two older sisters often visited him at his college lab.

datafile

Born: 1976

Place of birth: United States

Field: Geology

Super SHEro for: Learning more about the materials deep inside our planet

Wendy became interested in science. She went to the Massachusetts Institute of Technology (MIT) to study materials science. This field looks at what different substances are made of.

After finishing college, Wendy was not sure what to do next. After visiting her father's lab again, she decided to study natural materials, such as magma, rocks, and crystals. She would take what she already knew about materials and use that to learn more about the insides of Earth. She moved to the University of Chicago and began studying the iron in Earth's core.

MIT is a world-leading college for engineers and inventors.

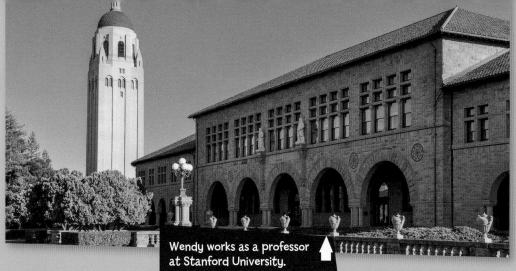

Wendy works as a professor at Stanford University.

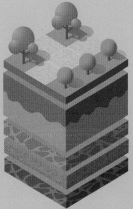

Next, Wendy moved to California, where she became a professor at Stanford University. From now on, she would combine research with teaching the next generation of scientists.

Wendy's work focuses on studying the materials deep within Earth. She uses X-rays and other techniques to study what they do under extreme conditions.

What's Your Story?

Throughout history, women scientists have often faced obstacles. Even today, in the United States only about a quarter of the scientists doing the same job as Wendy are women, and women of color are much rarer.

Have you ever been discouraged from an activity or a dream because of who you are?

Deep inside Earth, the temperature and **pressure** are very high. Materials behave differently down there than they would at the surface. In Wendy's lab, she and her team try to recreate what it is like inside the planet. Thanks to the research she leads, we now understand more about how Earth's core formed from hot iron.

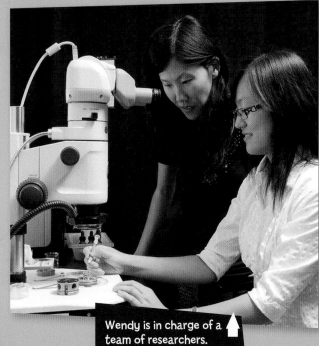

Wendy is in charge of a team of researchers.

Did You Know?

Earth is made of different layers. The **crust** is a hard outer layer that surrounds the planet like an eggshell. Beneath it is a thick layer of liquid magma called the mantle. A hot core is at Earth's center. The outer core is liquid metal and the inner core is solid.

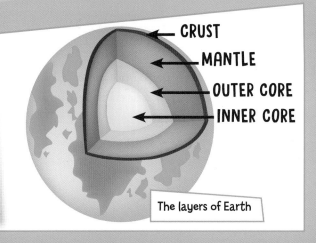

CRUST
MANTLE
OUTER CORE
INNER CORE

The layers of Earth

Wendy's work helps us understand the planets in our solar system.

In 2015, Wendy was part of a team that made another discovery. The team found specks of pure carbon inside ancient rocks. Almost always, carbon like this in nature is left there by living things. The rocks were 4.1 billion years old. This discovery meant that there might have been living things on Earth much earlier than scientists had thought before.

Wendy also worked with a team that learned to make diamonds from crude oil! Her discoveries help create new materials and inventions, including green technology that does not damage nature.

As Wendy learns more about our home planet, she is also helping to find ways to protect it in the future! **Wendy's amazing discoveries show there is still a lot for us to learn about Earth and its inside.**

New materials will be needed in the future to use clean fuels, such as hydrogen (H_2).

What Would You Do?

Wendy started off studying one subject and ended up switching to another, where she's been very successful.

Would you be willing to change your career path to learn something new?

What list of different careers would you choose?

SUPER SHEROES OF SCIENCE

Understanding **Earth** WEATHER

June Bacon-Bercey

June Bacon-Bercey
(United States, 1928-2019)

June Bacon-Bercey grew up in Wichita, Kansas. She was interested in weather from a young age and decided to study **meteorology** at college. As a Black woman she faced **discrimination**. At university in Los Angeles one of her science professors told her to switch to learning about cooking instead!

But June did not give up. She is believed to have been the first American Black woman to get a degree in meteorology. She was also the first female TV meteorologist in the United States, working at a station in Buffalo, New York. In 1977, June set up a college fund to help other women to study meteorology.

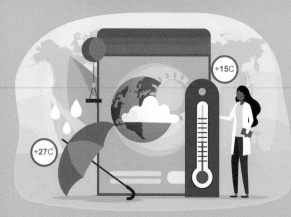

+15C

+27C

Rocío Caballero-Gill

The geologist Rocío Caballero-Gill was born in Lima, Perú. She investigates what Earth's climate was like a long time ago. She is particularly interested in the time when woolly mammoths were alive. Rocío examines mud on the ocean floor to find clues about what Earth was like back then. She describes herself as "a geo-detective" who looks at clues left behind in old ocean mud! Rocío has also set up the Geolatinas group to encourage young Latinas to become earth scientists.

Understanding
Earth
OCEAN FLOOR

Rocío Caballero-Gill
(Perú, born in the late 1980s)

SUPER SHEROES OF SCIENCE

Marie-Anne Paulze Lavoisier

Understanding Earth CHEMICALS

With her husband, the French chemist Antoine Lavoisier, Marie-Anne discovered how animals use oxygen in the air to stay alive. The Lavoisiers wrote a book together in 1789 that was a turning point in the history of science. Marie-Anne included very clear drawings so other chemists could understand the work.

Marie-Anne Paulze Lavoisier
(France, 1758-1836)

Inge Lehmann

Understanding Earth EARTH'S CORE

This Danish scientist discovered that Earth has a solid inner core. She found it by studying the way the big vibrations from earthquakes traveled through Earth. This showed that Earth's hot metal core is not completely liquid all the way through. It has a ball of solid metal spinning inside it.

Inge Lehmann
(Denmark, 1888-1993)

Florence Bascom

Florence Bascom's parents encouraged her to go to college, where she studied geology. Because she was a woman, she had to sit behind a screen during lectures to keep her separate from the male students.

In 1896, Florence became the first woman to be hired as a geologist by the US Geological Survey. This is a government agency that studies the landscape of the United States. Florence worked mostly in the Appalachian Mountains. She also worked as a professor in Pennsylvania, teaching female geologists. In 1930, Florence became the vice president of the Geological Society of America.

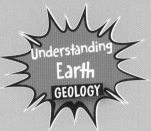

Florence Bascom
(United States, 1862-1945)

SUPER SHEROES OF SCIENCE

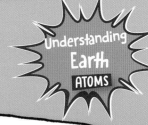
Understanding Earth
ATOMS

Lise Meitner

Lise Meitner was an Austrian physicist. In 1938, working with her nephew Otto Frisch in Berlin, she discovered nuclear fission. This is when the nucleus of one atom splits to form two smaller ones. Soon after, Lise, who was Jewish, moved to Sweden to escape the Nazis, who had taken over Germany and Austria.

Fission was later used to make atomic bombs, the most powerful weapons ever made. Lise refused to help make them. She didn't want her discovery to be used like this. In 1944, another researcher, Otto Hahn, received the Nobel Prize for discovering fission, and Lise was ignored! After her death, a new element was named meitnerium in her honor.

Lise Meitner
(Austria, 1878-1968)

Understanding
Earth
UNDERSEA MOUNTAINS

Marie Tharp

Marie Tharp was the first person to make a map of the seabed of the Atlantic Ocean. She wasn't allowed to sail on research ships because she was a woman. Instead, she took the information gathered by her research partner and turned it into a map. It included her greatest discovery: a 40,000-mile-long (65,000-km-long) chain of underwater mountains that almost circles Earth!

Marie Tharp
(United States, 1920–2006)

Sau Lan Wu

Understanding
Earth
PARTICLES

Sau Lan Wu is fascinated by the tiny particles that make up atoms and radiation. She works at the Large Hadron Collider (LHC) to search for them. The LHC is a vast machine in Switzerland that smashes particles together at very high speeds and records what happens next. Sau Lan's team helped discover a new particle called the Higgs boson. This mysterious particle is what gives atoms their heaviness.

Sau Lan Wu
(United States, born 1940s)

TimeLine

Here are some highlights in the history of understanding Earth.

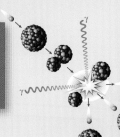

Florence Bascom is elected vice president of the Geological Society of America.

Lise Meitner publishes her work on nuclear fission.

Scientists suggest that all substances are made from tiny units called atoms.

Marie and Pierre Curie discover the elements radium and polonium.

| 1789 | 1803 | 1856 | 1898 | 1911 | 1930 | 1936 | 1939 |

Marie-Anne Paulze Lavoisier helps publish a book full of discoveries that change chemistry forever.

Eunice Newton Foote shows that gases in the air can change Earth's temperature.

Inge Lehmann discovers that Earth's core has two layers – one solid and one liquid.

Marie Curie becomes the first person ever to win two Nobel Prizes when she is awarded the prize for chemistry.

June Bacon-Bercey becomes the first female meteorologist to present the weather on television.

Katia Krafft is killed alongside her husband, Maurice, while studying an eruption at Mount Unzen in Japan.

Wendy Mao helps to discover evidence that there may have been simple life on Earth 4.1 billion years go.

Tennessine is the last element to be discovered.

| 1954 | 1970 | 1977 | 1991 | 1997 | 2010 | 2012 | 2015 |

Nuclear fission is used to make electricity for the first time.

Lise Meitner becomes the second female scientist (after Marie Curie) to have a chemical element named in her honor.

Sau Lan Wu's team helps to find a new particle, the Higgs boson.

Marie Tharp publishes the first complete map of the Atlantic Ocean seabed.

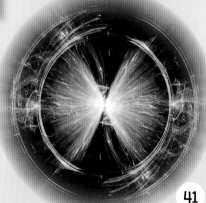

1. June Bacon-Bercey

Buffalo, New York

June was born and raised in Kansas, but her first television job was for a station in Buffalo.

2. Florence Bascom

Bryn Mawr, Pennsylvania

Florence set up the Department of Geology at Bryn Mawr, a women's college where she trained many female geologists.

3. Rocío Caballero-Gill

Virginia

Originally from Perú, Rocío is now based in Virginia, where she researches samples taken from the ocean floor.

4. Marie Curie

Paris, France

After leaving Poland, Marie spent the rest of her career based in Paris.

5. Eunice Newton Foote

Seneca Falls, New York

Eunice lived in Seneca Falls, the site of a women's rights convention, when she carried out her research.

6. Katia Krafft

Stromboli, Italy

Katia traveled the world, but Stromboli was the site of the first eruption that she visited with her husband, Maurice.

7. Marie-Anne Paulze Lavoisier

Paris, France

After marrying Antoine Lavoisier, Marie-Anne settled in Paris, where they built an early chemistry laboratory.

Atlantic Ocean

Pacific Ocean

N

8. Inge Lehmann
Copenhagen, Denmark
Inge did seismological research in Denmark and Greenland and was based in Copenhagen for most of her career.

10. Lise Meitner
Berlin, Germany
Lise carried out her nuclear research with Otto Frisch in Berlin before being forced to move to Sweden to escape the Nazis.

11. Marie Tharp
New York
Marie worked at the Lamont Geological Observatory in New York State.

rctic cean

pe

4.

7.

8.

10.

12.

6.

Asia

Pacific Ocean

Africa

Indian Ocean

Australia

Southern Ocean

12. Sau Lan Wu
Geneva, Switzerland
Sau Lan found evidence for the Higgs boson particle while working at the Large Hadron Collider on the border between France and Switzerland.

9. Wendy Mao
Stanford, California
Since 2007, Wendy has been a professor at Stanford University.

Words of Wisdom

Read the inspirational words of these
Super SHEroes of Science and remember:
You can become a Super SHEro, too!

Marie Curie

❝ It was like a new world opened to me, the world of science, which I was at last permitted to know in all liberty. ❞

❝ The fascination of any search after truth lies ... in the pursuit [chase], where all the powers of the mind are absorbed in the task. ❞

Florence Bascom

Katia Krafft

❝ [An eruption is] beautiful, it's aesthetic, it's also powerful - very, very powerful. Like a sea when you have a storm, it's the same. And it's because you are so small, and no longer something important, that it's wonderful. ❞

❝ I got a D in home economics and an A in thermodynamics. ❞

June Bacon-Bercey

Wendy Mao

" My work is exciting for me because it involves things that people haven't seen before. "

" Science makes people reach selflessly for truth; it teaches people to accept reality, with wonder and admiration, not to mention the deep joy and awe that the natural order of things brings to the true scientist. "

Lise Meitner

" I had a blank canvas to fill with extraordinary possibilities, a fascinating jigsaw puzzle to piece together. "

Marie Tharp

Glossary

asbestos (as-**bes**-tuhs) a heat-resistant mineral

atmosphere (**at**-muhs-*feer*) the layer of gases that surrounds Earth

atom (**at**-uhm) tiny building blocks that make up all substances

carbon dioxide (dye-**ahk**-side) a colorless gas released when fossil fuels such as coal, oil, and gas are burned

climate change (klye-**maht** chaynj) changes in the weather that are happening because of human activity

crater (**kray**-tur) a large hollow that forms the mouth of a volcano

crust (kruhst) the hard, rocky outer layer of Earth

discrimination (dis-*krim*-i-**nay**-shuhn) unfair treatment of others based on differences in things such as gender or race

element (**el**-uh-muhnt) one of the basic substances that cannot be broken down into other substances

geologist (jee-**uh**-lah-jist) a person who studies Earth

greenhouse effect (**green**-hous i-**fehkt**) the increased trapping of heat in the atmosphere, due to a buildup of certain gases

magma (**mag**-muh) melted rock beneath the surface of Earth

meteorology (*mee-tee-uh-**rah**-luh-jee*) the study of weather

Nobel Prize (no-**bell** pryz) a top prize awarded for achievements in science, writing, and peacemaking

particle (**pahr**-ti-kuhl) a small object that is usually combined to make a substance

physicist (**fiz**-i-sist) a person who studies the science of matter and energy, and of their relationship

pressure (**presh**-ur) a measure of how hard something is being squeezed

radiation (ray-dee-**ay**-shuhn) the giving off of energy in the form of waves or particles

radioactivity (ray-dee-oh-**ak**-tiv) a process where atoms fall apart

uranium (yu-**ray**-nee-uhm) a radioactive metal

vulcanologist (vuhl-can-**uhl**-oh-jist) a volcano scientist

Index

Further Reading

Amson-Bradshaw, Georgia. *Brilliant Women: Pioneers of Science and Technology.* London: Wayland, 2019.

Ignotofsky, Rachel. *Women in Science: 50 Fearless Pioneers Who Changed the World.* Berkeley, California: Ten Speed Press, 2016.

Katz, Susan B. *The Story of Marie Curie.* New York: Rockridge Press, 2020.

Lawlor, Laurie. *Super Women: Six Scientists Who Changed the World.* New York: Holiday House, 2019.

Nelson, Jo. *Destination: Planet Earth.* London: Wide Eyed Editions, 2018.

About the Author

Nancy Dickmann grew up reading encyclopedias for fun, and after many years working in children's publishing, she now has her dream job as a full-time author. She has had over 200 titles published so far, mainly on science topics, and finds that the best part of the job is researching and learning new things. One highlight was getting to interview a real astronaut to find out about using the toilet in space!

About the Consultant

Isabel Thomas is a science communicator and American Association for the Advancement of Science award-winning author. She has degrees in Human Sciences from the University of Oxford and in Education Research from the University of Cambridge, where her academic research focused on addressing inequalities in aspiration and access to science education and careers.